AF067394

World of Whales

Gray Whales

by Eliza Leahy

Bullfrog Books

Ideas for Parents and Teachers

Bullfrog Books let children practice reading informational text at the earliest reading levels. Repetition, familiar words, and photo labels support early readers.

Before Reading
- Discuss the cover photo. What does it tell them?
- Look at the picture glossary together. Read and discuss the words.

Read the Book
- "Walk" through the book and look at the photos. Let the child ask questions. Point out the photo labels.
- Read the book to the child, or have him or her read independently.

After Reading
- Prompt the child to think more. Ask: Orcas hunt gray whale calves. How do gray whale calves stay safe?

Bullfrog Books are published by Jump!
5357 Penn Avenue South
Minneapolis, MN 55419
www.jumplibrary.com

Copyright © 2024 Jump! International copyright reserved in all countries. No part of this book may be reproduced in any form without written permission from the publisher.

Library of Congress Cataloging-in-Publication Data

Names: Leahy, Eliza, author.
Title: Gray whales / by Eliza Leahy.
Description: Minneapolis, MN: Jump!, Inc., [2024]
Series: World of whales | Includes index.
Audience: Ages 5–8
Identifiers: LCCN 2022055537 (print)
LCCN 2022055538 (ebook)
ISBN 9798885245920 (hardcover)
ISBN 9798885245937 (paperback)
ISBN 9798885245944 (ebook)
Subjects: LCSH: Gray whale—Juvenile literature.
Classification: LCC QL737.C425 L43 2024 (print)
LCC QL737.C425 (ebook)
DDC 599.5/22—dc23/eng/20221208
LC record available at https://lccn.loc.gov/2022055537
LC ebook record available at https://lccn.loc.gov/2022055538

Editor: Katie Chanez
Designer: Emma Almgren-Bersie

Photo Credits: Nature Picture Library/Alamy, cover; Gregchapel0312/Dreamstime, 1; Andrei Stepanov/Dreamstime, 3; Alexander Machulskiy/Shutterstock, 4; Mark Conlin/VWPics/Alamy, 5; olon/Shutterstock, 6–7, 23tm; 4FR/iStock, 8–9, 23tr; Tory Kallman/Shutterstock, 10; Visual&Written SL/Alamy, 11; Rostislav Stefanek/Dreamstime, 12; Flip Nicklin/Minden Pictures/SuperStock, 12–13, 23br; Gerald Corsi/iStock, 14–15, 23tl; NOAA Fisheries, 16, 23bm; David Fleetham/Alamy, 17, 23bl; Wirestock Creators/Shutterstock, 18–19; BIOSPHOTO/Alamy, 20–21; FPLV/iStock, 24.

Printed in the United States of America at Corporate Graphics in North Mankato, Minnesota.

Table of Contents

Along the Ocean Floor	4
Parts of a Gray Whale	22
Picture Glossary	23
Index	24
To Learn More	24

Along the Ocean Floor

A gray whale swims in the ocean.

Its fins help.

fin

The whale is named for its color.

Its skin is gray.

Parts can be white.

Barnacles stick to it.

barnacles

It comes up for air.

It breathes with blowholes.

It dives.

It swims along the ocean floor.

It opens its mouth.
It scoops mud.
Why?
Tiny animals live in it.

13

baleen

Baleen strain mud and water out.

Food stays in.

Yum!

The whale swims to warm water.
It swims in a pod.

pod

Moms have calves.

calf

Look out!

An orca hunts.

The pod keeps the calves safe.

They swim close to shore.

Stay safe!

Parts of a Gray Whale

Gray whales can be up to 50 feet (15 meters) long. That is longer than a school bus! Take a look at the parts of a gray whale.

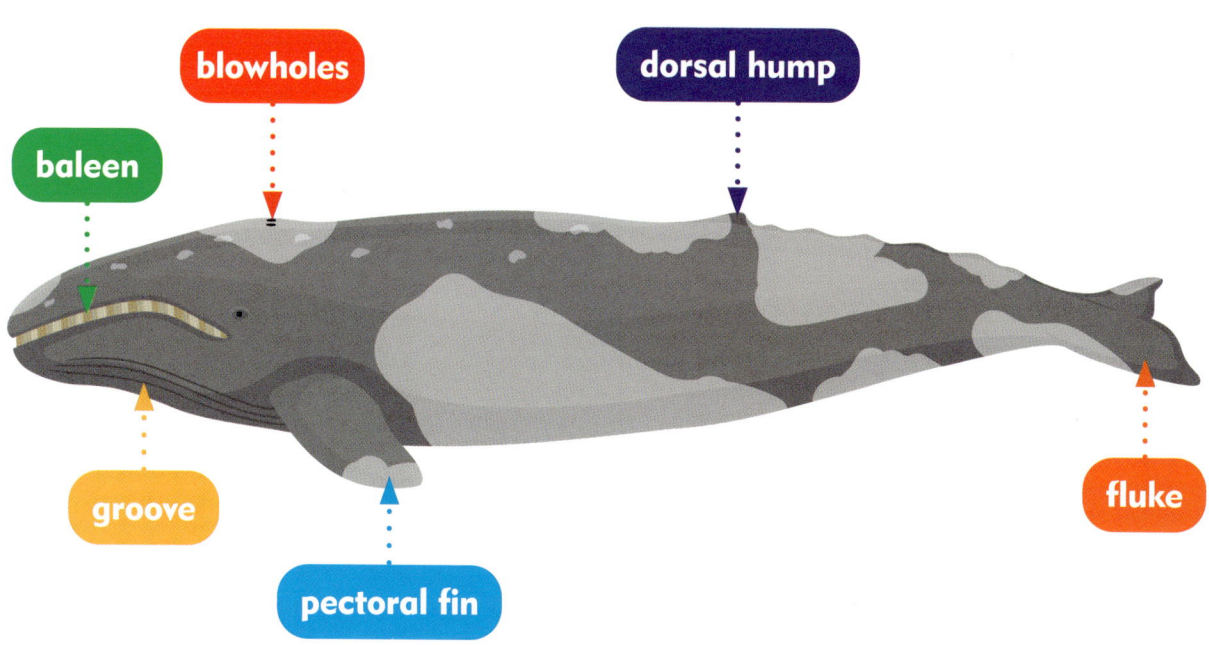

Picture Glossary

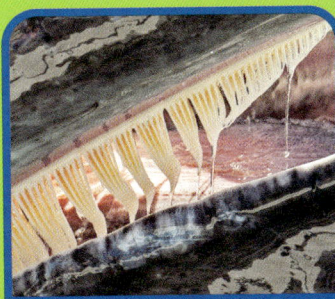

baleen
Plates in a whale's mouth that filter water and food.

barnacles
Small shellfish that attach to underwater surfaces.

blowholes
Nostrils on top of whale and dolphin heads used for breathing.

calves
Young whales.

pod
A group of whales.

strain
To separate solids out of liquids.

Index

baleen 15
barnacles 6
blowholes 9
calves 17, 20
color 6
dives 10

fins 5
food 15
mud 12, 15
orca 19
pod 16, 20
swims 4, 11, 16, 20

To Learn More

Finding more information is as easy as 1, 2, 3.
❶ Go to www.factsurfer.com
❷ Enter "graywhales" into the search box.
❸ Choose your book to see a list of websites.